THE 1920s
THROUGH THE DEC
eureka!
BY SARA GREEN

***Eureka!*** books turn real stories into unforgettable experiences. This nonfiction imprint sparks curiosity, encourages critical thinking, and engages middle-grade readers. *Eureka!* books empower young minds to explore the stories of the real world, one fascinating fact at a time. Unravel the power of knowledge and lifelong learning with *Eureka!*

This edition first published in 2026 by Bellwether Media, Inc.



Library of Congress Cataloging-in-Publication Data

LC record for The 1920s available at: https://lccn.loc.gov/2025021821



Editor: Christina Leaf Designer: Brittany McIntosh Series Designer: Andrea Schneider

Printed in the United States of America, North Mankato, MN.

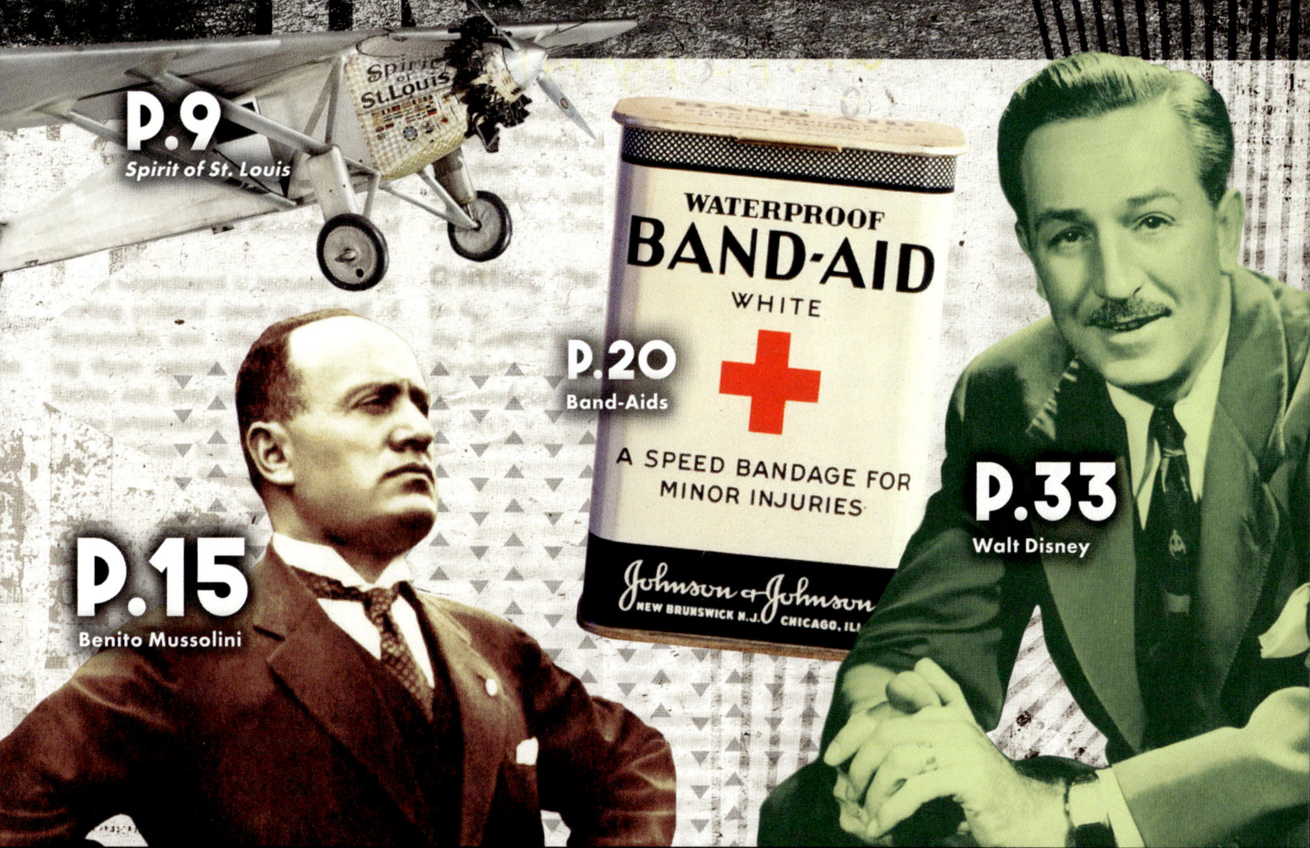


# TABLE OF CONTENTS

# WELCOME TO THE 1920s!

School is over for the day. The students wander out to the schoolyard. Some play a quick game of jacks as they wait for the school bus. The bus's noisy engine announces its arrival. It is more modern than the horse-drawn carriage the kids used to ride! One boy climbs onto one of the bus's wooden benches. Just then, it starts to rain. A tarp overhead keeps the kids dry. A Ford Model T passes the bus and gives a friendly honk. The boy waves. The Model T is the bee's knees!

At home, the boy greets his mother in the kitchen. Split pea soup simmers on the enamel stove. Maybe she made icebox cake for dessert! The boy changes out of his flat cap and **knickerbockers** and heads outside to do chores. His jobs are to feed the chickens and gather corn cobs used to heat the stove. After dinner, the family listens to the radio in the living room. One station is playing a newly popular type of music called jazz. The boy's parents kick up their heels to dance the Charleston, the latest dance craze. The 1920s are filled with new ideas!

TRANSPORT
909
SPEED 30 M.P.H.

# WHAT HAPPENED IN THE 1920s?

The 1920s are often called the "Roaring Twenties" due to the growth and optimism that defined the decade. World War I ended in 1918, and by 1920, a deadly flu **pandemic** had been contained. Both events claimed the lives of tens of millions of people. With these miserable events behind them, people were ready for better times. The thriving postwar economy created widespread prosperity. Many people owned appliances, telephones, and radios for the first time. The mass production of automobiles also made cars affordable for more people. People flocked to movie theaters and danced to jazz, a style of music sweeping the country. Prohibition sought to curb immoral behavior by banning alcohol.

Industrialization led to the growth of cities and shifting **demographics**. By 1920, more Americans lived in cities than in rural areas for the first time ever. This continued through the decade. During the Great Migration, many African Americans moved to urban areas in the North, Midwest, and West to find jobs and escape the South's **racism** and **segregation**. Women also gained new freedoms and rights with the 19th Amendment.

The glorious prosperity came to a halt at the end of the decade when the stock market crashed. The Roaring Twenties were over.

JAZZ PERFORMERS

## SWEET INVENTIONS

Baby Ruth bars, gummy bears, and Reese's Peanut Butter Cups were all invented in the 1920s. Dubble Bubble, the world's first bubble gum, was introduced in 1928. It was colored pink because that was the only food coloring available in the factory!

# HOW MUCH?

1 GALLON GAS
30 CENTS

THE NEW YORK TIMES
(daily national edition in New York)
2 CENTS (1920) | 5 CENTS (1929)

1 GALLON MILK
60 CENTS

MOVIE TICKET
15 CENTS

CANDY BAR
3 CENTS (1920)
5 CENTS (1929)

BOTTLE OF COKE
5 CENTS

LOAF OF BREAD
7 CENTS

DOZEN EGGS
47 CENTS

# HISTORY

## UNITED STATES HISTORY

The Roaring Twenties were marked by many revolutionary events. Much of the decade was affected by the 18th Amendment, known as Prohibition. The ratification of the 19th Amendment in 1920 was also important. It gave white women the right to vote. In 1927, a movie called *The Jazz Singer* debuted. It was the first full-length movie with spoken dialogue!

Many tragic events also happened in the 1920s. The Tulsa Race Massacre in 1921 was among the worst incidents of racial violence in United States history. The Great Mississippi Flood of 1927 was one of the U.S.'s most destructive floods. The decade ended with the stock market crash on October 29, 1929. This event, known as Black Tuesday, crippled the American economy and set off the **Great Depression**.

WOMEN VOTING FOR THE FIRST TIME

THE JAZZ SINGER

WALL STREET ON BLACK TUESDAY

# PROHIBITION

Prohibition began in 1920. It was a nationwide ban on the production, sale, and transportation of alcohol. It aimed to promote traditional American values and reduce crime. However, Prohibition was unsuccessful. Secret bars called speakeasies became popular. People also began making alcohol at home. In 1933, Congress passed the 21st Amendment to end Prohibition.

speakeasy

Al Capone

# ORGANIZED CRIME

Prohibition led to the rise of organized crime built on the illegal production, transport, and sale of alcohol. By 1927, notorious Chicago gangster Al Capone was earning more than $60 million a year from the illegal alcohol trade. In 1929, gang violence in Chicago led to a deadly shooting on Valentine's Day. It became known as the St. Valentine's Day Massacre.

# SOARING HIGH!

In 1927, pilot Charles Lindbergh made the first successful solo transatlantic flight. He flew 3,600 miles (5,794 kilometers) from New York City to Paris in his small plane, the *Spirit of St. Louis*. He became an instant celebrity! On June 18, 1928, Amelia Earhart became the first woman to ride in a plane that flew across the Atlantic Ocean.

*Spirit of St. Louis*

# UNITED STATES POLITICS

Three Republicans occupied the White House during the 1920s. Warren G. Harding was elected in 1920, beating James M. Cox. He campaigned on a return to normalcy after World War I. Harding promised to limit government involvement and help businesses grow. However, his administration was riddled with corruption. Its biggest scandal was called Teapot Dome. A member of Harding's administration took bribes and **kickbacks** from oil companies. President Harding died in office in 1923 and was succeeded by Vice President Calvin Coolidge.

President Warren G. Harding

## ELECTION SHOWDOWN: 1920 PRESIDENTIAL ELECTION

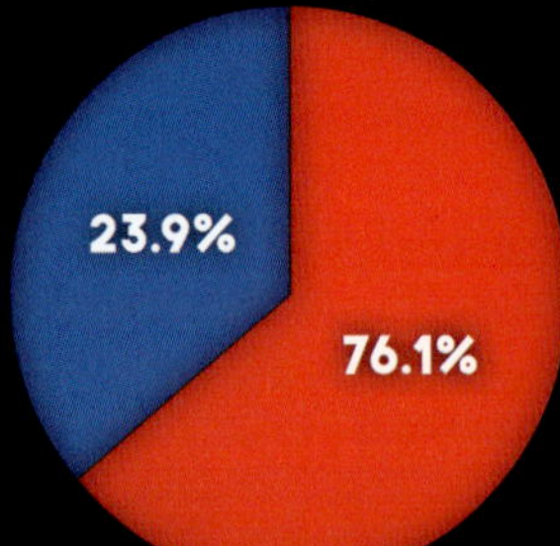


ELECTORAL VOTES

President Coolidge was known for his quiet, almost lazy, attitude. Under his leadership, the Immigration Act of 1924 was signed. It placed severe restrictions on people immigrating from certain countries, including Japan, Egypt, and many Eastern European nations. That year, Congress also passed a law that made all Native Americans citizens of the U.S. In 1928, President Coolidge joined Germany, France, and 12 other nations in signing the Kellogg-Briand Pact. It was an agreement to outlaw war. When his first term ended, Coolidge chose not to run again. Herbert Hoover, who had never held an elected position before, was elected president in 1928.

CALVIN COOLIDGE

SIGNING THE KELLOGG-BRIAND PACT

**PRESIDENTIAL PETS**

**President Coolidge was an animal lover. He owned dogs, cats, birds, and even a raccoon named Rebecca during his time in office. He also received twin lion cubs, a wallaby, and a pygmy hippo as gifts!**

HERBERT HOOVER

SPOTLIGHT ON:

# THE STOCK MARKET CRASH OF 1929

The U.S. economy reached an all-time high during the 1920s. The stock market was booming! People of all income levels began to **speculate** in the stock market, thinking it was a sure way to make money. Those with lower incomes invested in the market with borrowed money. This strategy is known as buying on margin. Confidence in the economy was high. People believed it might grow forever!

Everything changed in September 1929 when stock prices started to decline. Investors who had bought on margin rushed to sell their stocks to pay off their debts. On Thursday, October 24, a selling panic began. Within three hours, the stock market lost $11 billion in value. Then on Tuesday, October 29, the stock market collapsed. Around $14 billion was lost on what was called Black Tuesday. Millions of people lost their life savings. Within a few months, countless businesses went **bankrupt**, leading to massive unemployment. Millions of people were left **destitute**. Many lost their homes and possessions. The U.S. sank into a period of economic hardship called the Great Depression. This global downturn would last for more than 10 years.

## MAKING HEADLINES

"Wall St. in Panic As Stocks Crash"

—*Brooklyn Daily Eagle*, October 24, 1929

"BILLIONS LOST IN NEW STOCK MARKET CRASH"

—*THE MILWAUKEE LEADER*, OCTOBER 28, 1929

"Check Wall Street Panic"

–*New York Daily News*, October 30, 1929

# WORLD HISTORY

The 1920s was a decade of reconstruction and change for many countries after the end of World War I. Several countries were hampered by struggles. Germany in particular faced huge economic burdens due to the costs of war and war payments demanded by the **Allies**. Unemployment skyrocketed and the inflation rate grew until German money became nearly worthless. Many Germans could not afford to buy food and other necessities.

The 1920s also saw a rise in global **extremist** political movements. The Red Army defeated the White Army in the Russian Civil War, leading to the formation of a new nation called the **Soviet Union**. The **fascist** leader Benito Mussolini created a dictatorship in Italy in 1925. A bloody civil war began to ravage China. The Nazi Party also began to gain strength in Germany.

Several countries gained independence during the decade. Ireland and Egypt achieved independence from the United Kingdom in the early 1920s. Turkey declared its independence in 1923 after the end of the **Ottoman Empire**.

FOOD LINE IN GERMANY

Soviet Union flag

## A ROYAL DISCOVERY

**The tomb of Egyptian pharaoh King Tutankhamen was discovered in 1922 by British archeologist Howard Carter.**

# LEAGUE OF NATIONS

An international organization called the League of Nations formed after World War I. Its purpose was to settle disputes between countries and avoid war. American President Woodrow Wilson helped create the League. However, Congress voted against joining to avoid getting drawn into European affairs. When the League had its first meeting in 1920, 42 nations had agreed to join, but the U.S. had not.

Adolf Hitler

# THE RISE OF THE NAZI PARTY

The National Socialist German Workers' Party, or Nazi Party, started in 1919. By 1921, Adolf Hitler had become the party's leader. He and his followers exploited people's fears to lure them into joining the party. They hated many groups, including Jewish people, gay people, and people with disabilities. In 1923, Hitler tried and failed to overthrow the German government. He was sentenced to prison for five years but served only nine months. The Nazi Party continued to gain members and soon began winning political seats in Germany's legislature.

# THE RISE OF FASCISM

Benito Mussolini started the Fascist Party in Italy in 1919. He wanted to return Italy to the glory of Rome. The party joined Italy's coalition government in 1921. By 1925, Mussolini ruled Italy and outlawed all other political parties. As dictator, Mussolini had control of the economy, schools, military, and courts. He often used violence to achieve goals and squash opponents. Mussolini was ousted in 1943.

Benito Mussolini

SPOTLIGHT ON:

# THE BIRTH OF THE SOVIET UNION

During the Russian Revolution of 1917, Communist leader Vladimir Lenin led a group called the Bolsheviks to overthrow the Russian monarchy. A civil war raged for several years between the Bolsheviks' Red Army and opposing forces called the White Army. The war was brutal. It claimed the lives of up to ten million people. The war ended with a Bolshevik victory.

In 1922, the Bolsheviks formed a new socialist state called the Union of Soviet Socialist Republics (USSR), or the Soviet Union. The founding republics were Russia, Ukraine, Belarus, and Transcaucasia, which included the modern countries of Georgia, Armenia, and Azerbaijan. In time, the Soviet Union would grow to consist of 15 republics.

After Lenin died in 1924, General Secretary Joseph Stalin rose to power. He forced farmers to join **collectives** to increase agricultural production. He also launched a series of Five-Year Plans to increase industrialization. Stalin transformed the Soviet Union from an **agrarian** society to an industrial and military superpower. By the end of the 1920s, Stalin had established a **totalitarian** rule. Those who **dissented** faced arrest, imprisonment, or even execution.

RED ARMY SOLDIERS

FARMING COLLECTIVE

SOVIET STEEL MILL IN 1948

# WHO'S WHO?

## VLADIMIR LENIN

### ROLE:

Leader of the Bolshevik Party and first head of state of the Soviet Union (1922 to 1924)

### KNOWN FOR:

The founder of the Russian Communist Party who led the Bolshevik Revolution and established the Soviet Union's one-party state governed by the Communist Party.

## JOSEPH STALIN

### ROLE:

Leader of the Soviet Union from 1924 until his death in 1953

### KNOWN FOR:

A dictator who implemented policies that modernized the Soviet Union into a world superpower through the use of brutality, terror, and mass imprisonment.

# SOCIAL CHANGES

The new urbanism and prosperity of the 1920s led to dramatic social changes in American culture. Traditional norms were questioned as new ideas about equality and individual freedoms arose. New laws also drove social change. After the 19th Amendment was ratified, women began to participate in politics in greater numbers. They pushed for reforms in labor, education, health care, and child welfare, leading to improvements that benefited millions of Americans.

The Indian Citizenship Act, passed in 1924, granted U.S. citizenship to all Native Americans. It gave Native Americans the legal protections and rights guaranteed by the Constitution. However, the act did not address many of the challenges faced by indigenous communities, including land policies and **discrimination**.

New York City in 1928

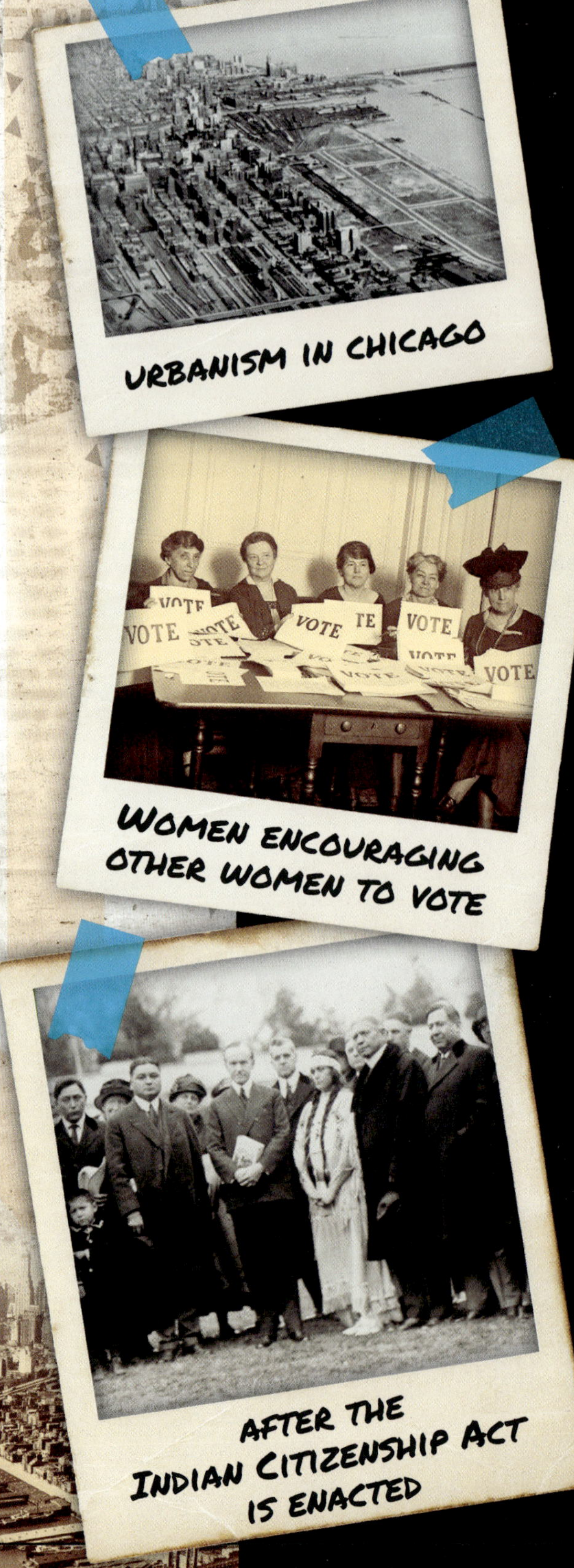

URBANISM IN CHICAGO

WOMEN ENCOURAGING OTHER WOMEN TO VOTE

AFTER THE INDIAN CITIZENSHIP ACT IS ENACTED

Heightened racial tensions during the decade led to the resurgence of a white **supremacist** group called the Ku Klux Klan (KKK). The KKK engaged in hateful acts to terrorize Black people, Catholics, Jews, immigrants, and other ethnic minorities.

Immigrants also faced new obstacles. Laws passed in the 1920s drastically reduced immigrants from certain regions. People from eastern and southern Europe were severely restricted. Asians were cut out entirely.

IMMIGRANTS REJECTED FROM ENTERING THE U.S.

Ku Klux Klan rally

# SCIENCE AND TECHNOLOGY

## TECHNOLOGICAL ADVANCEMENTS

Many products were invented or improved during the 1920s and became fixtures in people's lives for the first time. This is largely due to mass production. In 1913, Henry Ford developed the first moving assembly line for rapidly building automobiles. By the mid-1920s, the Ford company was building 9,000 Model Ts daily. This kept prices relatively low. In 1924, new Model Ts cost around $300. By 1929, more than 23 million automobiles were cruising on American roads! Mass production also boosted ownership of electrical appliances, including vacuum cleaners, refrigerators, and washing machines.

vacuum cleaner

### BAND-AID

**WHAT IS IT?:**
A sticky piece of disposable cloth or plastic used to cover and protect a cut or scrape on a person's skin

**INVENTOR:**
Earle Dickson

**YEAR INVENTED:**
1920

**EFFECT ON DAILY LIFE:**
Has helped people easily dress and protect wounds for more than 100 years

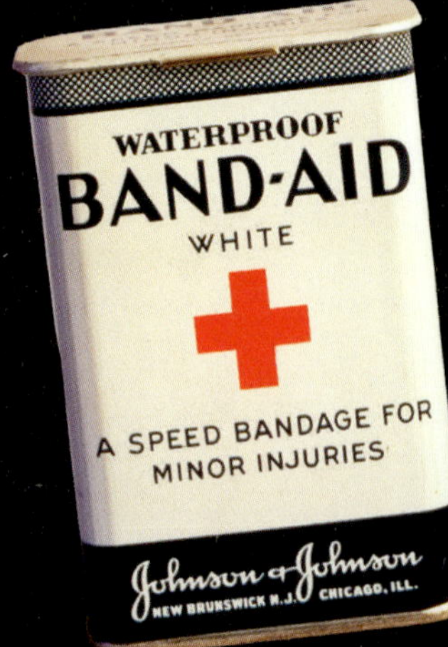

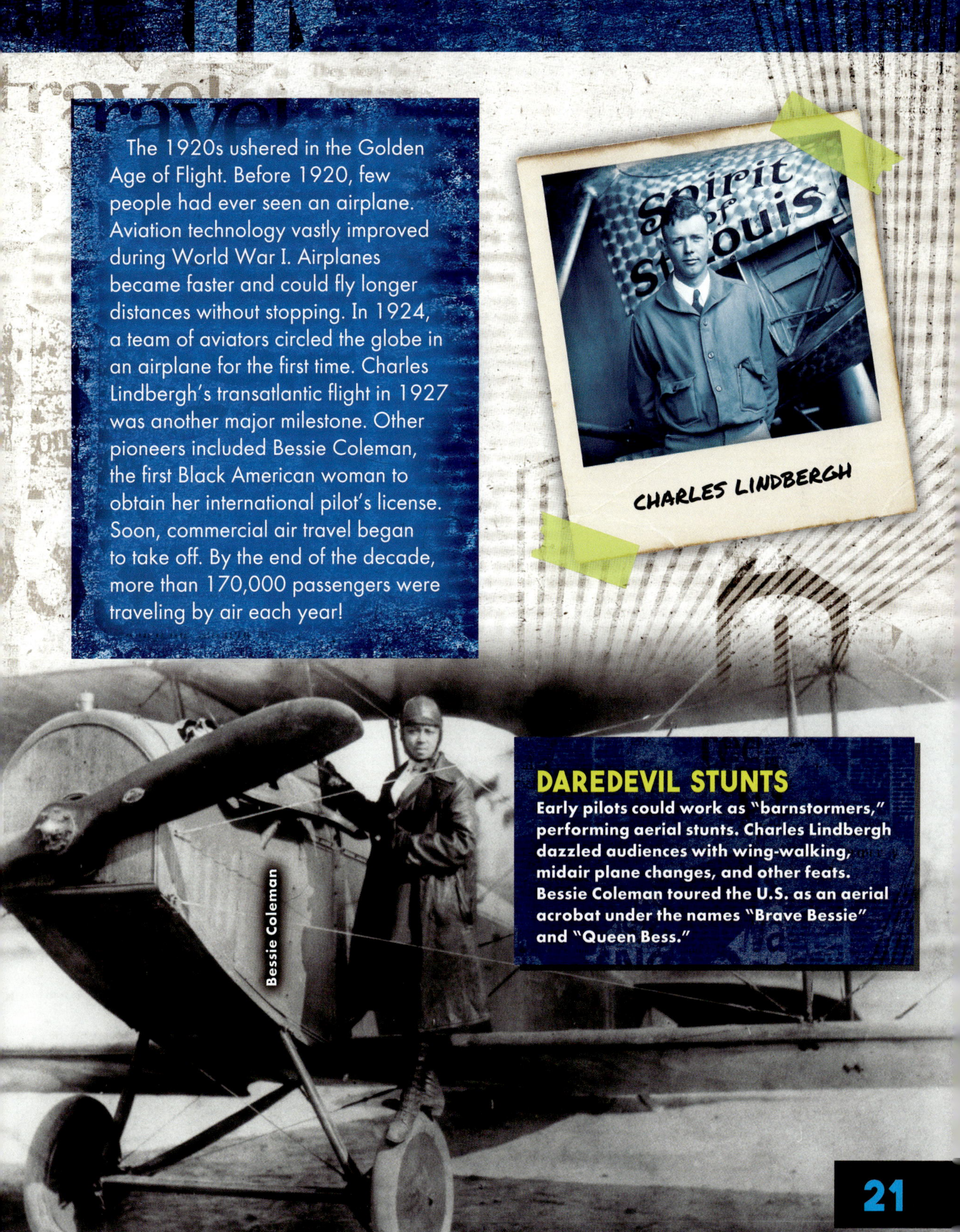


The 1920s ushered in the Golden Age of Flight. Before 1920, few people had ever seen an airplane. Aviation technology vastly improved during World War I. Airplanes became faster and could fly longer distances without stopping. In 1924, a team of aviators circled the globe in an airplane for the first time. Charles Lindbergh's transatlantic flight in 1927 was another major milestone. Other pioneers included Bessie Coleman, the first Black American woman to obtain her international pilot's license. Soon, commercial air travel began to take off. By the end of the decade, more than 170,000 passengers were traveling by air each year!

CHARLES LINDBERGH

Bessie Coleman

## DAREDEVIL STUNTS

**Early pilots could work as "barnstormers," performing aerial stunts. Charles Lindbergh dazzled audiences with wing-walking, midair plane changes, and other feats. Bessie Coleman toured the U.S. as an aerial acrobat under the names "Brave Bessie" and "Queen Bess."**

# MEDICAL ADVANCEMENTS

Many important medical advancements were made in the 1920s. A lung disease called tuberculosis (TB) was a leading cause of death in the early 1900s. After 13 years of research, French scientists developed a successful vaccine called BCG in 1921. BCG is still used today to protect people from tuberculosis. Also in 1921, Canadian researchers discovered insulin, a life-saving hormone for people with diabetes. It was used to treat diabetes for the first time in 1922 with great success. In 1928, Scottish **bacteriologist** Alexander Fleming accidentally discovered penicillin. Some of his Petri dishes had become contaminated with mold. To his surprise, the mold was killing the bacteria! Fleming named the mold penicillin. Scientists developed it into one of the world's first antibiotics. Over time, the TB vaccine, insulin, and penicillin have saved countless lives.

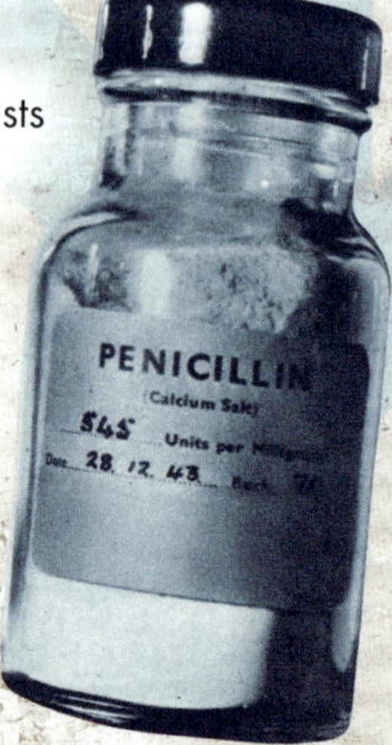

TUBERCULOSIS WARD

STUDYING INSULIN

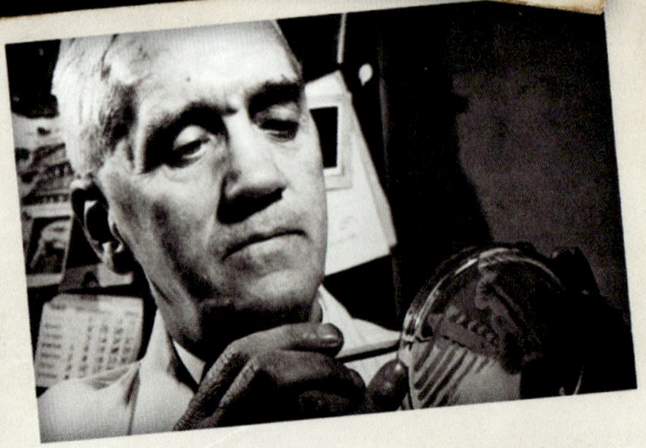

ALEXANDER FLEMING

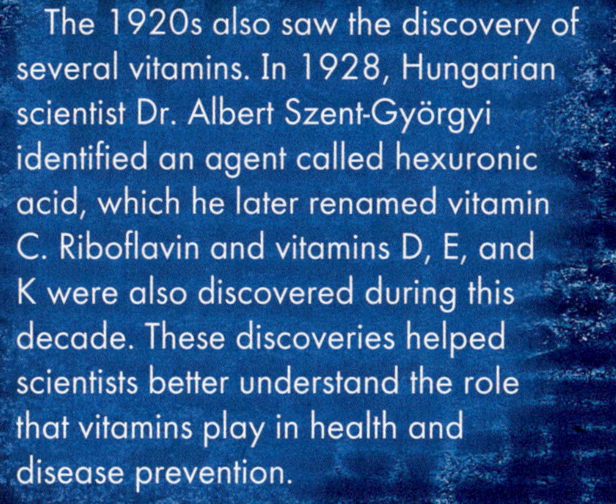

The 1920s also saw the discovery of several vitamins. In 1928, Hungarian scientist Dr. Albert Szent-Györgyi identified an agent called hexuronic acid, which he later renamed vitamin C. Riboflavin and vitamins D, E, and K were also discovered during this decade. These discoveries helped scientists better understand the role that vitamins play in health and disease prevention.

DR. ALBERT SZENT-GYÖRGYI

## SCOPES MONKEY TRIAL

**By the 1920s, Charles Darwin's theory of evolution was taught in schools across the country. In March 1925, the state of Tennessee passed a law that prohibited teaching evolution in public schools. John Scopes, a high school science teacher in Dayton, Tennessee, defied this law. He gave a classroom lecture on Darwin's theory and was arrested. This led to a highly publicized trial called the Scopes Monkey Trial.**

**John Scopes with his defense team**

# DAILY LIFE

## LIFE IN THE '20s

The dramatic changes of the 1920s greatly affected many people's daily lives. Large numbers of young people began embracing a new sense of freedom and moved to cities seeking jobs, entertainment, and excitement. Going to movies, dancing at nightclubs, and listening to the radio were popular pastimes. Leisure driving was another favorite activity. People drove around towns and the countryside just to be seen!

More women than ever before began entering the workforce, typically as teachers, nurses, factory workers, or clerks. However, no matter their occupation, women were generally expected to quit their jobs after marrying to focus on housekeeping and childcare. Despite widespread employment discrimination, Black workers earned higher wages in the North than they did in the South. Housing discrimination led to the formation of tight-knit Black communities in northern cities such as New York, Philadelphia, and Detroit.

By the early 1920s, more children were attending school. Higher enrollments led to the creation of larger schools with many classrooms and teachers. Outside of school, many students held jobs to help support their families. Rural kids often worked in fields, while city kids worked in factories or mines, sold newspapers, or shined shoes.

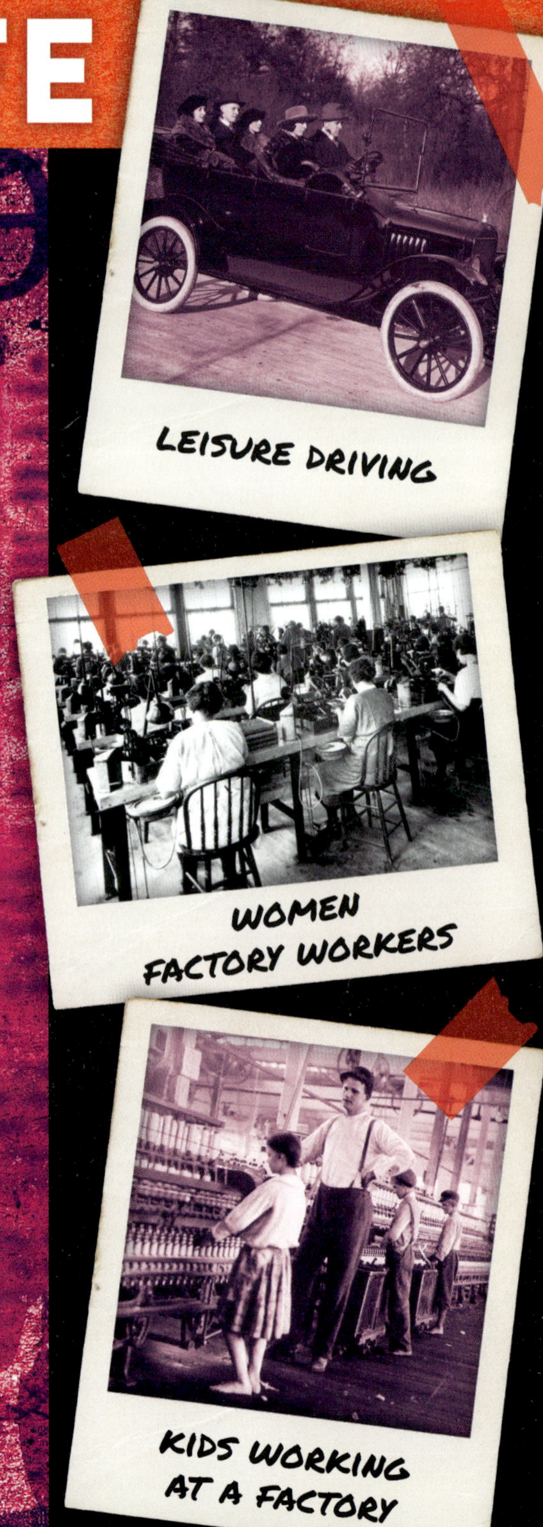

LEISURE DRIVING

WOMEN FACTORY WORKERS

KIDS WORKING AT A FACTORY

# 1920s SLANG

The Cat's Pajamas

the best

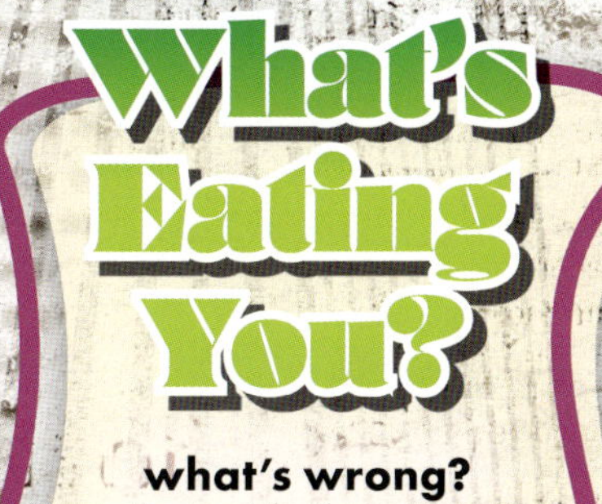

# FASHION TRENDS

The 1920s saw big changes in fashion. Restrictive dresses and **corsets** were out. Simpler, looser, and more comfortable clothing was in! Sportswear for women became popular. Hemlines of women's dresses rose from mid calf-length in 1920 to knee-length in 1927. The boyish flapper look became the height of fashion. The look included short, straight, sleeveless dresses and bobbed hair. Beaded headbands and cloche hats made the look extra chic! The rise of the film industry also influenced fashion choices. Women sought to look like Clara Bow, Greta Garbo, and other movie stars. Many used curling irons to create a hairstyle called the Marcel wave. Recent changes to makeup and beauty products also made it easier to copy the stars' glamorous looks.

classic flapper look

## ALL STARS

**Converse released the Chuck Taylor All Stars sneaker in 1922 after basketball player Charles "Chuck" Taylor joined the company. It was the first celebrity-endorsed athletic shoe!**

Men also adopted a more casual look in the 1920s. Many opted to wear shorter jackets that featured pinstripes, plaid, and other patterns. Long jackets with tailcoats were reserved for formal occasions. Knickerbockers and sweaters became sporty staples. The decade's most stylish hat was the fedora. Flat caps and porkpie hats were also popular. Many men completed their outfits with canes, a popular fashion accessory in the 1920s.

# PRODUCTS AND TOYS

The rise of mass production in the 1920s had a huge impact on the toy industry. Mass-produced toys were cheaper to make and easier to market. For the first time, kids could find the same toys on store shelves across the country. Most toys required children to use their imaginations to create and play!

## YO-YO

**The first yo-yos were created long ago in ancient Greece and China. In the 1920s, a bellhop in a California hotel named Pedro Flores entertained guests by doing tricks with a yo-yo. Flores began his own company to manufacture yo-yos in 1928.**

## TRAIN SETS

**The 1920s is remembered as a golden age of model trains. Toy trains became more realistic, and many had electric motors. However, train sets were very expensive. Only wealthy families could afford to have them.**

## PEDAL CAR

**Pedal cars were simplified models of full-sized cars driving the roads at the time. Some had working headlights, foldable rear seats, and starter cranks. Pedal cars were expensive to buy, so many people made their own versions.**

## RAGGEDY ANN AND ANDY

The Raggedy Ann doll debuted in 1918. In 1920, her little brother, Raggedy Andy, was introduced. The dolls come to life in a series of books called the Raggedy Andy Stories by Johnny Gruelle. They share many exciting adventures together!

## LINCOLN LOGS

Lincoln Logs hit shelves in 1924. John Lloyd Wright created a toy construction set containing notched pieces of wood that could be interlocked. Wright named his creation Lincoln Logs after Abraham Lincoln. Each set came with instructions on how to build cabins like Lincoln's boyhood home!

## ERECTOR SET

The Erector Set, launched in 1913, was a construction toy aimed at boys. It included nuts, bolts, and beams in multiple sizes. In 1924, the Erector Set was redesigned to include new parts and a motor. Kids could build more complex structures, including Ferris wheels, trains, and steam shovels.

## RADIO FLYER WAGON

The Radio Flyer Wagon was created by Antonio Pasin, a craftsman living in Chicago. Pasin started building and selling wooden toy wagons in 1917. In 1927, Pasin began making steel wagons. He used the name Radio Flyer after recent popular inventions.

## A.C. GILBERT CHEMISTRY SET

The A.C. Gilbert Company released its first chemistry set in 1923. The set came in a case that contained jars of chemicals, test tubes, and small tools. Also included was a booklet containing easy instructions on how to do experiments.

# ARTS AND ENTERTAINMENT

## PUBLICATIONS

The literature of the 1920s reflected the changing social landscape. Authors explored themes such as personal freedom, racial tensions, and the role of women in society. Artists and writers would gather together at **salons** to exchange ideas and discuss political and social issues.

Many celebrated poets lived during the 1920s. T.S. Eliot's masterpiece "The Waste Land" is considered one of the most important poems of the 20th century. Black writers such as Langston Hughes and Claude McKay wrote powerful poems about the Black experience during the Harlem Renaissance.

Crossword puzzles experienced a huge craze in the 1920s. They appeared in newspapers, magazines, and even inspired a Broadway musical! The *Little Orphan Annie* comic strip debuted in the *New York Daily News* in 1924. It ran in newspapers until 2010. *The Adventures of Tintin*, a popular comic strip featuring Tintin and his fearless dog, Snowy, debuted in 1929 in Belgium.

## READING REC

**TITLE:**
***WINNIE-THE-POOH***

**AUTHOR:**
A.A. Milne

**YEAR PUBLISHED:**
1926

**SUMMARY:**
The story is about a lovable bear named Winnie-the-Pooh and his adventures with friends Piglet, Eeyore, Owl, Rabbit, Kanga, and Roo in the Hundred Acre Wood.

## MAGAZINES

Many popular magazines started in the 1920s. *TIME* and *Reader's Digest* provided summaries of news and other topics for busy readers. *The Brownies' Book* became the first magazine intended for Black children. *Better Homes and Gardens*, *The New Yorker*, and *Architectural Digest* also debuted.

## THE LOST GENERATION

The Lost Generation was a group of American writers that included F. Scott Fitzgerald, Ernest Hemingway, and Gertrude Stein. The writers had become disillusioned with American society and its materialistic values after World War I. Many fled to Paris, France, a city considered to be an artistic and literary hotspot. *The Great Gatsby* by F. Scott Fitzgerald and *The Sun Also Rises* by Ernest Hemingway are two Lost Generation classics.

## CHILDREN'S BOOKS

Many classic children's books were published in the 1920s. The mysteries and adventures in The Box-Car Children and The Hardy Boys series delighted generations of young readers. *The Velveteen Rabbit* and *The Story of Doctor Dolittle* inspired children's imaginations with stories of wonder and companionship. Their characters remain favorites today.

## THE HARLEM RENAISSANCE

Many of the Black Americans who moved north during the Great Migration settled in a New York City neighborhood called Harlem. It became the center of a creative movement called the Harlem Renaissance. This movement showcased Black culture and explored themes of racism, slavery, and Black identity. Jean Toomer, Nella Larsen, and Zora Neale Hurston were among the most prominent writers of the Harlem Renaissance.

## THE GOLDEN AGE OF DETECTIVE FICTION

The Golden Age of Detective Fiction is a period in the 1920s and 1930s when crime novels surged in popularity. Agatha Christie helped popularize the genre. Her first novel, *The Mysterious Affair at Styles*, was published in 1920. Other influential Golden Age novelists included Dorothy L. Sayers, Anthony Berkeley, and Dashiell Hammett.

# MOVIES

Movie attendance soared during the 1920s as people found themselves with more disposable income. Around 50 million people a week were going to the movies by 1925!

All movies were silent until 1926. That year, studios experimented with **synchronized** sound effects and music. The arrival of spoken dialogue in 1927 revolutionized the movie industry. Movie theaters across the country were soon wired with sound to show talking pictures, or "talkies." Box office sales soared! Talkies also changed the acting industry. Some silent film stars transitioned easily to the new technology. Those with voices or skills less suited to sound found their careers ruined at the end of the decade.

## THE JAZZ SINGER

**In 1927, Warner Brothers Pictures released *The Jazz Singer* starring Al Jolson. It became the first feature-length talking picture with synchronized dialogue. Although the movie is still largely silent, the few hundred spoken words in the movie riveted audiences and led to the end of the silent film era.**

## AT THE BOX OFFICE

### TOP-GROSSING FILMS OF THE 1920s

- ***The Big Parade*** **(1925)**
- ***The Singing Fool*** **(1928)**
- ***Ben-Hur: A Tale of the Christ*** **(1925)**
- ***The Four Horsemen of the Apocalypse*** **(1921)**
- ***Something to Think About*** **(1920)**
- ***The Covered Wagon*** **(1923)**
- ***The Jazz Singer*** **(1927)**
- ***The Kid*** **(1921)**
- ***The Gold Rush*** **(1925)**
- ***Way Down East*** **(1920)**

*The Big Parade*

# ACADEMY AWARDS

The Academy of Motion Picture Arts and Sciences was founded in 1927. It presented the first Academy Awards in 1929 at a ceremony held at the Hollywood Roosevelt Hotel. The awards ceremony had an audience of around 270 people. It lasted about 15 minutes.

# CHARLIE CHAPLIN

Charlie Chaplin rose to stardom making silent films. He was best known for his character the Tramp, with his sad eyes, mustache, baggy pants, and cane. Movie audiences adored him. Chaplin was the top box office attraction of his time. *The Gold Rush*, released in 1925, was one of the most successful movies of the silent film era.

*The Gold Rush*

# HOLLYWOOD, CALIFORNIA

In the 1910s, moviemakers began to flood a small village called Hollywood. The land was cheap and the sunny weather allowed filmmakers to shoot outside year-round. By 1920, Hollywood had become the film capital of the world! In 1923, real estate developers put up a sign advertising the Hollywoodland neighborhood. The sign quickly became a popular landmark!



# WALT DISNEY →

In 1923, Walt Disney and his brother Roy started the Disney Brothers Cartoon Studio, Hollywood's first animated cartoon studio. In 1928, the studio released *Steamboat Willie*, the first animated cartoon with synchronized sound. The cartoon introduced Mickey Mouse and Minnie Mouse. The movie was a huge hit. It skyrocketed Mickey Mouse to fame!

Walt Disney

# TELEVISION AND RADIO

The 1920s saw a rapid rise of commercial radio and radio stations. People gathered around the radio to listen to news, comedy shows, and dramas. Music performances were another staple of radio programming. People tuned in to listen to jazz, dance bands, and other popular music of the time. Broadcasts of sporting events also became popular as the decade progressed.

Television technology, still in its early days, continued to advance, too. The decade set the stage for major developments to follow!

KDKA reporting on the 1920 presidental election

## KDKA

**On November 2, 1920, KDKA in Pittsburgh, Pennsylvania, became the first commercial radio station to make a broadcast. The station announced the live results of the 1920 presidential election between Warren G. Harding and James M. Cox. People no longer had to wait to read the newspaper to keep up with current events. By 1922, there were 576 licensed radio broadcasters across the country.**

## GRAND OLE OPRY

***Grand Ole Opry* is a country music broadcast that started in 1925. Originally called the *WSM Barn Dance*, it showcases live country and folk music performances from Nashville, Tennessee. Today, it ranks as the world's longest-running radio program!**

John Logie Baird's 1926 demonstration

## MECHANICAL TELEVISION

Inventors John Logie Baird and Charles Francis Jenkins developed a system called mechanical television during the 1920s. Mechanical televisions used rotating discs to capture and show images on screens. In 1926, Baird was one of the first people to demonstrate any kind of television to the public.

## PHILO TAYLOR FARNSWORTH

Inventor Philo Taylor Farnsworth developed the first working electronic camera tube in 1927. That year, he made the first electronic television transmission, which was a straight line displayed on a screen. This transmission led to the development of modern television.

Philo Taylor Farnsworth with a camera tube

## VARIETY SHOWS

Variety shows were a popular form of radio entertainment in the 1920s. They featured musical performances, comedy sketches, and other entertainment. *The Eveready Hour* debuted in 1923. It was sponsored by Eveready Battery's parent company, the National Carbon Company. It was the first variety show with commercial sponsorship.

radio

# MUSIC

The 1920s was an exciting time for music. People were ready to put the dark years of World War I behind them. They wanted upbeat, fun music. A relatively new genre called jazz quickly became one of the most popular music genres of the 1920s. The decade is often called the Jazz Age due to the genre's widespread popularity!

New dance styles celebrated the sense of freedom that arose during the decade, especially among young people. Fast-paced dances such as the Charleston and the Lindy Hop swept the nation. Advances in technology helped bring music to wider audiences. Ownership of radios and phonographs surged throughout the decade. More people than ever were listening to music in their homes!

## JAZZ

**The earliest jazz was developed by Black Americans in the late 19th century in New Orleans. Its musical styles were inspired by ragtime music, the blues, and brass marching bands. Dixieland was one of the earliest forms of jazz. This lively music is played by small ensembles. Its hallmark is collective improvisation, where musicians play their own melodies at the same time.**

## 1920s PLAYLIST

- ***Crazy Blues***
  **Mamie Smith (1920)**
- ***Whispering***
  **Paul Whiteman & His Ambassador Orchestra (1920)**
- ***Swanee***
  **Al Jolson (1920)**
- ***Down Hearted Blues***
  **Bessie Smith (1923)**
- ***The Prisoner's Song***
  **Vernon Dalhart (1924)**
- ***Rhapsody in Blue***
  **George Gershwin (1924)**
- ***Blue Skies***
  **Josephine Baker (1927)**
- ***My Blue Heaven***
  **Gene Austin (1927)**
- ***St. James Infirmary Blues***
  **Louis Armstrong (1928)**
- ***Ain't Misbehavin'***
  **Fats Waller (1929)**

Bessie Smith

## THE BLUES

The blues is a musical form that began in the southern U.S. after the Civil War. Blues records specifically aimed at Black audiences helped spread the genre to wider audiences in the 1920s. Female singers like Bessie Smith, Ma Rainey, and Mamie Smith helped make the blues a national sensation.

## LOUIS ARMSTRONG

Louis Armstrong was a jazz trumpet virtuoso, singer, and composer. His trumpet skills and gravelly singing voice made him one of the world's most famous musicians. Armstrong was also known for scat singing, a style of vocal improvisation where singers make up nonsense syllables or use their voices to imitate instruments. He recorded many hit records and inspired generations of musicians to come!

## JOSEPHINE BAKER

Josephine Baker was a Black American dancer and singer. In 1925, Baker began performing in music halls in France. Her talent and beauty skyrocketed her to superstardom. She is remembered as one of the most successful performers in French history.

## GEORGE GERSHWIN

George Gershwin was a celebrated American pianist and composer. His music often combined classical styles with jazz and other popular music. Gershwin's groundbreaking composition *Rhapsody in Blue* premiered on February 12, 1924, in New York's Aeolian Hall to widespread acclaim. Gershwin also composed many popular songs for Broadway and musical theater.

## CHARLESTON →

The Charleston is among the most famous dances of the 1920s. It is fast paced with a lot of twisting and kicking. The dance is based on the Juba, a dance that enslaved Africans brought to Charleston, South Carolina. The Great Migration helped spread the Charleston dance across the country.

# U.S. SPORTS

The 1920s ushered in the Golden Age of Sports in the U.S. Spectator sports grew as a major form of entertainment. People had more leisure time to follow sports. Radio broadcasts also helped sporting events reach a wider audience. Fans could follow the excitement as it happened rather than wait to read scores in a newspaper!

Professional baseball was the decade's most popular sport, followed closely by boxing and college football. The National Football League (NFL) began in 1920 and got its current name in 1922. Other sports, such as tennis and golf, were also drawing new fans. Many top athletes, such as Babe Ruth and Jack Dempsey, achieved fame. Some became national and even international heroes!

## MVP

**NAME:**
**BABE RUTH**

**SPORT:**
Baseball

**YEARS PLAYED:**
1914 to 1935

**TEAMS:**
Boston Red Sox, New York Yankees, and Boston Braves

**KNOWN FOR:**
A powerful hitter who set many records, including the most home runs in a season in 1927 with 60 and the most career home runs with 714, both of which lasted for many years.

## NEGRO LEAGUES

The Negro Leagues were organized professional baseball leagues made up of Black American and Latin American players. The first, the Negro National League, was founded in February 1920. These organizations arose due to racial segregation that prevented players of color from participating in Major League Baseball (MLB) and other white professional leagues. The leagues featured many talented players. Some, including Satchel Paige and Oscar Charleston, became baseball legends.

## RED GRANGE

Harold "Red" Grange, nicknamed the "Galloping Ghost," was a University of Illinois running back known for his speed. Red turned pro in 1925 and joined the Chicago Bears. Red was football's first superstar. He drew thousands of new fans to the sport and helped bring professional football into the national spotlight.

## BABE RUTH

George Herman "Babe" Ruth Jr. was already a star when he began playing for the New York Yankees in 1920. In 1923, he was named Most Valuable Player in the American League. Yankee Stadium opened that same year in the Bronx. Ruth attracted huge crowds to the new stadium and amazed his fans with his power hitting. He led the American League in home runs from 1926 to 1931, hitting a record 60 home runs in 1927.

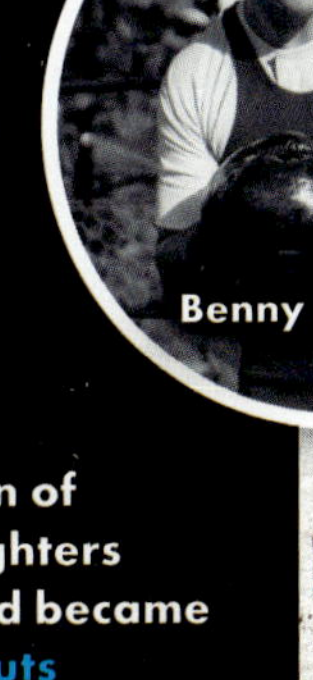
Benny Leonard

## BOXING

The first sporting event to be broadcast over the radio was a boxing match in April 1921. Boxing quickly attracted the attention of the general public. Fighters such as Benny Leonard became household names. Bouts between Jack Dempsey and Gene Tunney earned more than $2 million!

## HORSE RACING

Man o' War, also known as Big Red, is considered one of the greatest racehorses of the 20th century. In 1920, he won all 11 races he entered, including the Preakness Stakes and the Belmont Stakes. He set seven track records and became the first North American Thoroughbred to earn more than $200,000 in total winnings.

## TENNIS

Tennis's popularity soared during the 1920s. Bill Tilden, known as "Big Bill" for his height, was the decade's most famous male player. He dominated the game from 1920 to 1926 and was the first American male to win Wimbledon. Helen Wills commanded the women's division. She became the world's first American female sports celebrity and ranks among the top female tennis players in history.

# GLOBAL SPORTS

Exciting international sporting events tested athletes around the world during the 1920s. A number of Olympic firsts happened in the decade. The 1920 Antwerp Games introduced the Olympic flag with its five rings and the Olympic Oath. Chamonix, France, hosted the first Winter Games in the French Alps in 1924. While the torch would come later, the 1928 Amsterdam Games started with a symbolic fire. The Olympics of this decade helped create goodwill and unity between different nations following the division caused by World War I. It helped lay the foundation for the development of many international sporting events to come!

## OLYMPICS OF THE 1920s

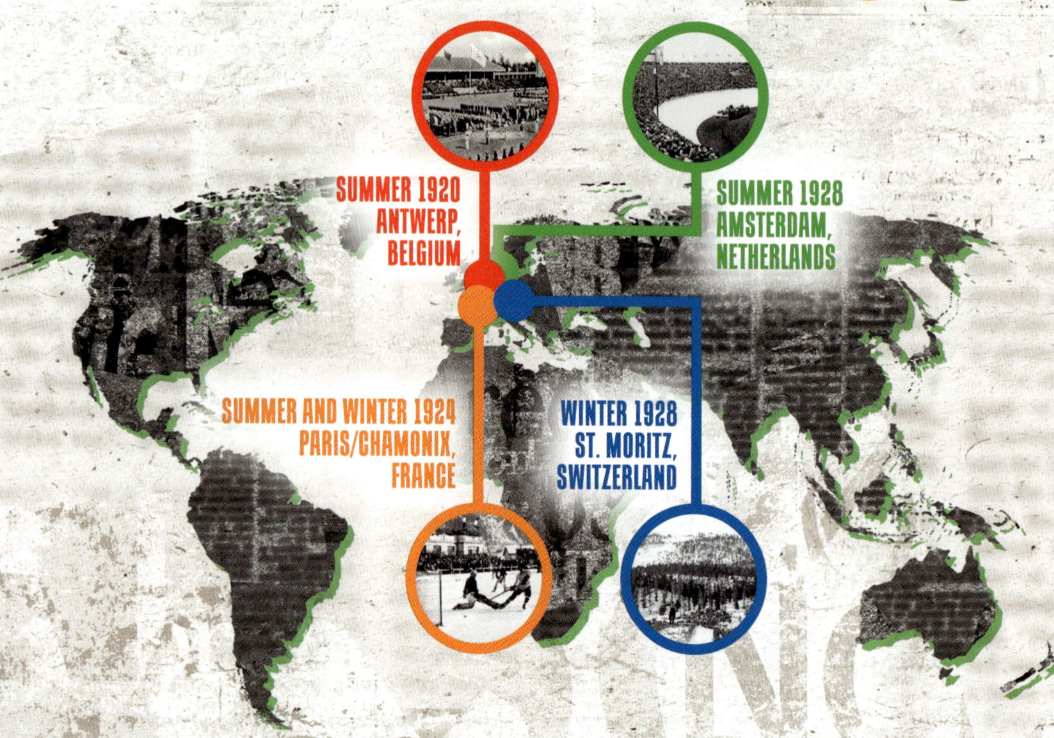

## 1920 SUMMER OLYMPICS

The 1920 Summer Olympics in Antwerp, Belgium, were the first Olympic Games held after World War I. More than 2,600 athletes representing 29 countries participated. Germany, Austria, Hungary, and other countries defeated in the war were excluded from the Games.

## 1924 WINTER OLYMPICS

The first Winter Olympic Games were held in 1924. Sixteen nations competed for medals in skiing, figure skating, ice hockey, and other winter sports in Chamonix, France. American speed skater Charles Jewtraw became the Winter Games' first gold medalist when he won the men's 500-meter speed skating event.

Charles Jewtraw

## GERTRUDE EDERLE

American swimmer Gertrude Ederle was one of the most famous athletes of the 1920s. She won one gold and two bronze medals at the 1924 Olympics. By mid-decade, Ederle held 29 amateur swimming records. She made history on August 6, 1926, when she became the first woman to swim across the English Channel.

## RYDER CUP

The Ryder Cup is a golf competition between the U.S. and Europe. The first event took place in June 1927 in Worcester, Massachusetts. An American team led by golf champion Walter Hagen played Great Britain, led by Ted Ray. Team USA beat Team Great Britain to win the first trophy!

## SONJA HENIE

Sonja Henie was a Norwegian figure skater who rose to fame at the age of 14. In 1927, she won her first of 10 world championships in a row. Henie won her first gold medal in the 1928 Winter Olympics. She revolutionized figure skating with her grace and athleticism. She later went on to become a professional ice skater and successful movie star.

## STANLEY CUP

In 1928, the New York Rangers became the second American hockey team to win the Stanley Cup championship. They beat the Montreal Maroons 3–2 to clinch the victory. This was the Rangers' first appearance in the Stanley Cup Finals. The trophy was originally given to the top Canadian team. The National Hockey League (NHL) took it over in 1926.

# TIMELINE

**JANUARY 10, 1920**
The League of Nations is formed, but the U.S. refuses to join

**JANUARY 17, 1920**
Prohibition begins

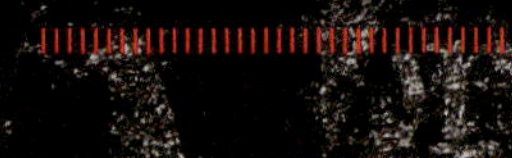

**AUGUST 18, 1920**
Ratification of the 19th Amendment grants women the right to vote

**SEPTEMBER 17, 1920**
The American Professional Football Association is formed and two years later changes its name to the National Football League

**NOVEMBER 2, 1920**
The first radio broadcast by KDKA in Pittsburgh is transmitted, in which Leo Rosenberg delivers live results from the presidential election between Warren G. Harding and James M. Cox

**MAY 31 TO JUNE 1, 1921**
The Tulsa Race Massacre takes place

**APRIL 7, 1922**
Interior Secretary Albert Fall accepts a bribe from an oil company, beginning the Teapot Dome Scandal

**MAY 5, 1922**
The construction of Yankee Stadium begins in New York City

**NOVEMBER 8 TO 9, 1923**
Adolf Hitler and the Nazi Party attempt to overthrow the German government in a failed coup d'etat

**JUNE 2, 1924**
Congress passes the Indian Citizenship Act

**DECEMBER 30, 1922**
The Soviet Union forms

**FEBRUARY 12, 1924**
George Gershwin's *Rhapsody in Blue* premieres at Aeolian Hall in New York

**JANUARY 25, 1924**
The first Winter Olympic Games begin in the French Alps in Chamonix, France

**MAY 26, 1924**
President Calvin Coolidge signs the Immigration Act into law

**OCTOBER 16, 1923**
Walt and Roy Disney found the Disney Brothers Cartoon Studio in Los Angeles, California

**JANUARY 5, 1925**
Nellie Tayloe Ross is inaugurated as the first woman governor in the U.S. in Wyoming

**APRIL 10, 1925**
*The Great Gatsby* by F. Scott Fitzgerald is published

**JULY 10, 1925**
The Scopes Trial begins

**NOVEMBER 28, 1925**
*Grand Ole Opry*, then known as the *WSM Barn Dance*, first airs

**OCTOBER 14, 1926**
*Winnie-the-Pooh* by A.A. Milne is published

**MAY 20, 1927**
Charles Lindbergh departs from Roosevelt Field, New York, to make the first solo transatlantic flight

**SEPTEMBER 7, 1927**
Philo Taylor Farnsworth makes the first successful electronic television transmission

**SEPTEMBER 30, 1927**
Babe Ruth hits his 60th home run of the season, a record that stands until 1961

### JUNE 18, 1928

As a passenger, Amelia Earhart becomes the first woman to fly across the Atlantic Ocean

### OCTOBER 29, 1929

The Wall Street crash of 1929 occurs, resulting in the Great Depression

### OCTOBER 6, 1927

*The Jazz Singer*, the first successful motion picture with synchronized dialogue, premieres

### NOVEMBER 18, 1928

Disney's *Steamboat Willie* opens, the first animated movie to feature Mickey Mouse

### SEPTEMBER 3, 1928

Alexander Fleming discovers a mold that stops bacteria growth, which he names penicillin

### MAY 16, 1929

The first Academy Awards ceremony takes place at the Hollywood Roosevelt Hotel in Hollywood, California

### 1928

H.B. Reese invents Reese's Peanut Butter Cups

# GLOSSARY

**agrarian**—an economy based on products grown on farmland

**Allies**—the countries that fought against Germany, Austria-Hungary, and Turkey during World War I

**bacteriologist**—a scientist who studies single-celled living things that usually live in plants and animals or in soil or water

**bankrupt**—unable to pay debts

**bouts**—sports matches

**coalition government**—a government formed jointly by more than one political party

**collectives**—large-scale farms owned by the state and operated by groups of farmers

**corsets**—tight, stiff undergarments worn by women to shape their waists and hips

**demographics**—characteristics that describe a population, such as age, race, and gender

**destitute**—extremely poor

**discrimination**—the act of treating someone unfairly because of race, gender, age, ability, or other differences

**dissented**—disagreed with the goals or methods of a government

**extremist**—views that are far outside of society's mainstream attitudes

**fascist**—related to a belief that a dictator should control the government and people's lives without any opposition

**genre**—a category of a kind of art based on style, form, or content

**Great Depression**—a time in world history when many countries experienced economic crisis; the Great Depression began in 1929 and lasted through the 1930s.

**improvisation**—the art of making up music on the spot

**kickbacks**—money given to someone in return for unethical or illegal behavior

**knickerbockers**—short, baggy pants that fit tightly below the knee

**Ottoman Empire**—a Turkish-led empire that ruled over a vast area of the Middle East, North Africa, and Eastern Europe from the 14th to early 20th centuries

**ousted**—removed from office

**pandemic**—an event in which an illness spreads over a large area to many people

**racism**—the belief that race is a fundamental part of human traits and that certain races are superior to others

**salons**—places where groups of people gather together to discuss intellectual topics

**segregation**—the act of separating people based on their race

**Soviet Union**—short for the Union of Soviet Socialist Republics; the Soviet Union is a former country in Eastern Europe and western Asia made up of 15 republics or states that broke up in 1991.

**speculate**—to make a risky investment with the hope of earning a large profit

**supremacist**—related to the belief that one race, religion, ethnicity, or other group is superior to all others

**synchronized**—happening together at the same time

**totalitarian**—a political system where the government has complete control over the lives of its citizens

**virtuoso**—someone who is extremely skilled at something

## WRITE ABOUT IT!

- Where do you see parallels in the 1920s to today? Choose one and draw comparisons between the two decades.
- What do you think society would be like today if mass production had never been invented?
- What do you think were the greatest challenges faced by Black Americans who headed north during the Great Migration?

# INDEX




The images in this book are reproduced through the courtesy of: PictureLux/ The Hollywood Archive/ Alamy Stock Photo, front cover (Baker), p. 37 (Baker); Stan Rohrer/ Alamy Stock Photo, front cover (Model T); Glasshouse Images/ Alamy Stock Photo, front cover (Ruth), pp. 3 (Mussolini), 15 (Mussolini); WikiJunkie/ Wikipedia, front cover (Prohibition); Veikk0.ma/ Wikipedia, front cover (equal rights); Flask/ Wikipedia, front cover (The Great Gatsby), p. 31 (top); OsvátA/ Wikipedia, front cover (jazz orchestra); National Air and Space Museum, pp. 3 (Spirit of St. Louis), 9 (Spirit of St. Louis); James Keyser/ Contributor/ Getty Images, pp. 3 (Band-Aids), 20 (Band-Aids); RGR Collection/ Alamy Stock Photo, pp. 3 (Walt Disney), 33 (Walt Disney); Patrick Jennings, p. 4 (jacks); The Washington Post/ Contributor/ Getty Images, p. 4 (icebox cake); ModelTMitch/ Wikipedia, p. 4 (Ford Model T); thislife pictures/ Alamy Stock Photo, p. 5; JP Jazz Archive/ Contributor/ Getty Images, p. 6 (top); BradReeseCom/ Wikipedia, p. 6 (bottom); Winai Tepsuttinun, p. 7 (gas); Photo Builder, p. 7 (NYT); Artiom Photo, p. 7 (milk); phive2015, p. 7 (bread); Alex Bogatyrev, p. 7 (eggs); AlenKadr, p. 7 (Coke); Bettmann/ Contributor/ Getty Images, pp. 8 (top), 9 (Capone), 13 (bottom), 17 (Stalin), 19 (all), 22 (insulin, Fleming), 23 (bottom), 26 (right), 27 (Bow), 34 (all), 35 (right), 38, 39 (all); George Rinhart/ Contributor/ Getty Images, pp. 8 (middle), 41 (Jewtraw); PhotoQuest/ Contributor/ Getty Images, pp. 8 (bottom), 18 (women voting), 24 (middle, bottom); Fæ/ Wikipedia, p. 9 (speakeasy); Heritage Images/ Contributor/ Getty Images, pp. 10, 16 (top); Everett Collection, p. 11 (Coolidge); Hulton Deutsch/ Contributor/ Getty Images, pp. 11 (Kellogg-Briand pact), 21 (top), 24 (top), 35 (left); brandstaetter images/ Contributor/ Getty Images, p. 11 (Hoover); Universal History Archive/ Contributor/ Getty Images, pp. 11 (pets), 37 (Armstrong); London Express/ Stringer/ Getty Images, p. 13 (top); FPG/ Staff/ Getty Images, pp. 14 (top), 40 (St. Moritz); zmotions, p. 14 (middle); ullstein bild Dtl./ Contributor/ Getty Images, p. 14 (bottom); Topical Press Agency/ Stringer/ Getty Images, p. 15 (League of Nations); ZUMA Press, Inc./ Alamy Stock Photo, p. 15 (Hitler); Chronicle/ Alamy Stock Photo, pp. 16 (middle), 22 (penicillin), 32 (right); Everett Collection Inc/ Alamy Stock Photo, p. 16 (bottom); Laski Diffusion/ Contributor/ Getty Images, p. 17 (Lenin); Keystone/ Stringer/ Getty Images, p. 18 (New York); Archive Collection/ Alamy Stock Photo, p. 18 (Chicago); Library of Congress, p. 18 (Indian Citizenship Act); Fotosearch/ Stringer/ Getty Images, p. 20 (left); Michael Ochs Archives/ Stringer/ Getty Images, p. 21 (bottom); Mirrorpix/ Contributor/ Getty Images, p. 22 (TB ward); PD Archive/ Alamy Stock Photo, p. 23 (top); xMarshall, p. 26 (left); Paul O'Connell, p. 27 (fedora); H. Armstrong Roberts/ ClassicStock/ Contributor/ Getty Images, p. 27 (Marcel wave); Bob Thomas/ Popperfoto/ Contributor/ Getty Images, p. 27 (knickerbockers); Pavel Skopets, p. 28 (yo-yo); John Henshall/ Alamy Stock Photo, p. 28 (train set); Motoring Picture Library/ Alamy Stock Photo, p. 28 (pedal car); Chris Willson/ Alamy Stock Photo, p. 29 (Lincoln logs); MediaNews Group/ Reading Eagle via Getty Images/ Contributor/ Getty Images, p. 29 (Raggedy Ann); Take Photo, p. 29 (wagon); A. A. Milne/ Wikipedia, p. 30; Ctac/ Wikipedia, p. 31 (bottom); John Springer Collection/ Contributor/ Getty Images, p. 32 (left); World History Archive/ Alamy Stock Photo, p. 33 (Chaplin); blestkater, p. 33 (Hollywood); Al Victor, p. 35 (bottom); Tekkol, p. 36; Michael Ochs Archives/ Handout/ Getty Images, p. 37 (Smith); Weegee(Arthur Fellig)/ International Center of Photography/ Contributor/ Getty Images, p. 37 (Charleston); Getty Images/ Staff/ Getty Images, p. 40 (Antwerp); Central Press/ Stringer/ Getty Images, p. 40 (Amsterdam); Hulton Archive/ Stringer/ Getty Images, p. 40 (Paris/Chamonix); Kirby/ Stringer/ Getty Images, p. 41 (Ederle); Tino Bandito, p. 41 (Stanley Cup); Domingo Saez, p. 42; magr80, p. 43; JimmyJoe87/ Wikipedia, p. 44 (left); PSchatzkin/ Wikipedia, p. 44 (right); HONG VO, p. 45 (left); WALT DISNEY/ RGR Collection/ Alamy Stock Photo, p. 45 (right).